Estate Planning and the Modern Family:
Old School Meets New School

Peter A. Moustakis, Esq.

ISBN-13: 978-1534615458

DEDICATION

To my late father, whose memory shall be eternal.

CONTENTS

INTRODUCTION

One of the most important decisions you can make in your life is how you want your possessions to be distributed after you pass away. Do you want certain possessions to go to specific family members? Do you have a close friend or two, or a trusted employee who you'd like to see get something meaningful from your estate? Would you like some of your assets to go to a charitable organization? Do you have a pet or pets who are almost like family members? How do you want them to be taken care of when you pass? You certainly don't want them to be neglected – or worse.

How you plan for your estate to be distributed and looked after once you pass is important, for many reasons. First, you don't want your family to be torn apart fighting over who gets what. In addition, you don't want the government to get a large chunk of your estate – all because you didn't make out a Last Will and Testament.

Planning for what happens to your possession when you pass away is called Estate Planning. It involves more than just making out a Last Will and Testament, which essentially is a distribution plan for your possessions after you pass away. Estate Planning also encompasses health care decisions, including who will speak for you should you become incapacitated and unable to make or express those decisions yourself.

Proper estate planning can accomplish many things. It can give you peace of mind, knowing that the appropriate people and organizations will acquire the possession you want them to acquire. It can save your family from a difficult, and possibly divisive, struggle to determine how to distribute your assets. It can help preserve your possessions so that the government does not take a disproportionate share of everything you worked so hard for in your lifetime. It can also help determine the quality of life you want, because you will have appointed someone to speak in your behalf, should you become seriously ill and unable to effectively communicate your wishes.

Estate planning has gone "new school" in a number of ways in recent years. First, the legal profession has walked away from estate planning documents filled with obtuse legalese and Latin words that are often hard to understand, and is increasingly using plain, everyday English. In addition, many attorneys are advising their clients to keep copies of their documents not only in paper form but also electronically, either on a mobile device, desktop computer or stored on "the Cloud." There are several reasons for this, not the least of which is that the documents are easier to access by those who need them, either when you pass or if you become incapacitated and unable to communicate your wishes.

This book is intended to give readers a broad overview of the estate planning process, from Old School to New School. It is intended to be used as an educational resources. This book is absolutely not a substitute for legal advice, nor should it be considered such.

DISCLAIMER

This book is intended to give readers a broad overview of the estate planning process in Massachusetts and New Hampshire. It is intended to be used as an educational resource only. This book is absolutely not a substitute for legal advice, nor should it be considered such, due to the constant changes in the laws and necessary application of those laws to an individual situation.

This book does not provide an exhaustive discussion of the matters discussed in it. Everyone's situation is unique, and every estate plan should be developed by an attorney after consultation with the individual or family. The material in this document is for informational purposes only and should not be considered legal advice. Before you make any decision that may have legal implications, you should consult with a qualified legal professional for specific legal advice tailored to your situation. Your possession of this document does not establish an invitation to enter into, and does not create an attorney-client relationship.

1

WHAT IS ESTATE PLANNING?

Estate Planning, essentially, is the process of deciding what will happen to your possessions when you pass away, and who will make financial and health care decisions for you if you are unable to make those decisions yourself. This process often includes a discussion of the tax ramifications of distributing property during your lifetime or at your death, as well as a discussion about the quality of life you wish to have.

The goal of any estate planning attorney is to work with a client to help him or her plan for the future by developing and implementing a structured, organized plan to deal with the client's estate and provide peace of mind to the client and the client's family. The kinds of documents you may need to have prepared depends on your situation and assets. Therefore the initial meeting between you and the attorney is critical in determining what your goals are and the proper way of achieving those goals. At the end of the meeting you should be presented with a list of options along with the advantages and disadvantages of those options based on your interests.

Here is a list of some of the commonly drafted documents during the estate planning process:

- Health Care Proxy
- Advance Directive
- HIPAA Release
- Durable Power of Attorney
- Will
- Trusts

Health Care Proxy

A Health Care Proxy is a legal instrument by which you appoint an individual to make medical decisions for you in the event you become incapacitated and are unable to make or communicate decisions for yourself. The Health Care Agent should be someone you believe will consult with your physician, weigh the benefits and risks of any treatment that may be available and will follow your expressed wishes in your Advance Directive.

Advance Directive

An Advance Directive, also known as a "living Will", is a set of instructions you give that specifies what actions should be taken on your behalf in the event that you are no longer able to make decisions due to illness or incapacity. Although, as current law stands, such a document is not legally binding in some states, including Massachusetts, it does provide the Health Care Agent with some guidance as to what your feelings are about these sensitive matters.

HIPAA Release

Under the Health Insurance Portability and Accountability (HIPAA) Act, a medical provider is required to have a patient's written authorization before releasing the patient's medical information or discussing the case with a Health Care Agent. A HIPAA Release Form is a document which authorizes the disclosure of your protected health information to the people who are listed in the document. The HIPAA Release often names the same individuals who are the agents in the Health Care Proxy.

Durable Power of Attorney

A Durable Power of Attorney is a legal instrument by which you can appoint another person to handle your financial affairs. If you become incapacitated without a valid Durable Power of Attorney in place, a court may have to decide who should manage your affairs. This process can be expensive and stressful.

Will

A Will is a legal document that is executed with certain formalities, and usually directs the disposition of your property at death. A Will includes the distribution of generalized personal property, specific gift dispositions to named persons or charities, estate administrative provisions and the naming of a personal representative or representatives and successors. It is important to note that joint accounts generally pass on death to the joint owner. Similarly, property with beneficiary designations will generally go to such designated beneficiary, and not necessarily to those named in the Will.

Trusts

Trusts can be used to do the following:

- Minimize estate taxes
- Avoid probate
- Care for animals

- Protect assets for a minor, disabled or spendthrift persons, and
- Protect assets from having to be used to pay for nursing home care

Not everyone actually needs a Trust; therefore it is important for you and the attorney to review what property you own, how you own it and how your family situation may determine whether a Trust is advisable to achieve your interests.

2

DO-IT-YOURSELF ESTATE PLANNING DOCUMENTS: A CAUTIONARY TALE

Do-It-Yourself legal websites have sprung up in recent years. Why bother with the expense and hassle of hiring a lawyer, some of these sites imply, when you can simply follow the online instructions and get everything you need to meet your legal and estate-planning needs? Here's the reality: If you use one of these Do-It-Yourself sites, you could wind up spending far more trying to correct or untangle the mistakes made when you relied on the site's boilerplate "one-size-fits-all" documents and advice than you would have if you had simply hired a competent estate planning lawyer in the first place. Or, perhaps even worse, your reliance on the documents and information on these sites could mean that your wishes, or the wishes of your loved ones, are not properly carried out.

What these online services offer are what is known as "Boiler Plate" documents. These are basic templates of documents that seem to fulfill many of your needs at once. This might sound like an ideal solution to spending money on legal fees, but in reality, the consequences of using these documents – rather than paying for legal advice and assistance tailored to your specific situation – could be disastrous.

A judge in Florida best summed up the folly of relying on Do-It-Yourself legal documents. She stated, in a case involving one of these documents prepared by an online service, that an individual could end up "...penny-wise and pound-foolish."

The court further stated:

"I therefore take this opportunity to highlight a cautionary tale of the potential dangers of utilizing pre-printed forms and drafting a will without legal assistance. As this case illustrates, that decision can ultimately result in the frustration of the testator's intent, in addition to the payment of extensive attorney's fees – the precise results the testator sought to avoid in the first place."

In that Florida case, a woman had an online legal-document service prepare her estate planning documents. What she did not realize was that the document failed to carry out her wishes the way she intended. In essence, the Will she prepared online distributed only a portion of her property to her intended beneficiaries and the remainder of her estate was left to individuals she did not want to inherit her property.

As a result, both the client and her intended beneficiaries lost out. The client's last wishes were not carried out the way she envisioned, and the intended beneficiaries did not receive the intended inheritance and were subject to additional legal fees by litigating the matter.

Here's another way to put this in perspective: You can go online and learn how to perform surgery on yourself, but would you want do it yourself rather than have a licensed, experienced surgeon perform the operation? Think of an attorney as a legal surgeon. An estate planning attorney has executed wills and other estate planning documents many times and knows how to develop a plan and execute the documents to meet your exact needs and desires.

3
THE FAMILY MEETING

Sowerby & Moustakis Law, PLLC has developed and refined a process called The Family Inheritance System that maps out what will happen as your life unfolds. This system gives you, and your loved ones, a clear picture of how your estate will be administered and how your assets and possessions will be distributed. The Family Inheritance System is an additional value to the traditional estate planning process that a client can participate in. Below are the first major components of the system.

The Family Inheritance System

1. *Consultation* – The initial consultation is free of charge to the client. At this meeting we discuss what the client's interests are and what the client would like to accomplish.
2. *Roadmap* – We devise an inheritance plan for the client based on the client's goals and interest and we explain to the client how we will achieve those interests.

3. *Plan Creation* – We collect and organize all of the information obtained through the client meetings and prepare the documents necessary to achieve the client's interests.
4. *Plan Execution* – The client signs and executes all the documents necessary to put the plan in place.
5. *Family Meeting* – The client can invite his or her personal representative, children or family to the office to discuss "what it might look like" when the client passes away.

The Family Meeting is the element that makes this system successful. The purpose of the Family Meeting is to gather together family members and fiduciaries of your estate plan to discuss what your estate plan is intended to do and what it might look like if you become incapacitated or pass away.

It's helpful to bring written descriptions of the following to the meeting:

- A listing and description of your assets
- The title of your assets
- Location of financial and legal documents
- An online digital accounts worksheet

The Family Meeting is not for everyone, but those who choose to participate find real value in sharing their wishes with family members so that there are no surprises in the future.

4

DEVELOPING A TEAM

OF TRUSTED ADVISORS

Whenever someone creates an estate plan or receives an inheritance, it makes sense for them to assemble a team of trusted advisors. The size of the estate or inheritance does not change the need to have a team of trusted advisors. It is always important to rely on the advice of experts who can help you make decisions that are right for you and your estate.

Such advisors may include:

- Attorney
- Certified Public Accountant
- Financial Advisor
- Life Insurance Agent
- Long Term Care Insurance Agent
- Disability Insurance Agent
- Supplemental Insurance Agent
- Commercial Real Estate Agent

- Residential Real Estate Agent
- Personal Lines Insurance Agent
- Mortgage Broker
- Bookkeeper
- Banker

5

NAMING FIDUCIARIES

As part of any estate plan you will need to select people to act as fiduciaries in different capacities. A fiduciary is a person (or a business like a bank or stock brokerage firm) who has the power and obligation to act for another (often called the beneficiary) under circumstances which require total trust, good faith and honesty.

Will

A Personal Representative is also known as an Executor and is a fiduciary that should be named under a Will. This is the person responsible for administering your estate upon your passing. Some of the responsibilities include, but are not limited to: securing your probate property; filing court paperwork on behalf of your estate; choosing whether or not to use an attorney to help with the process; and making dispositions to the beneficiaries under the Will. The person you choose should be someone who you believe will be alive when you have passed away. Most people tend to choose a spouse to act in such capacity.

A Guardian and Conservator may also need to be nominated if you have minor or incapacitated children. A guardian is a person who will care for a minor or incapacitated person and make the day-to-day decisions if both of the child's parents have passed away. You can name anyone who you feel will act in your child's best interest in such capacity. For example you can choose a sibling or a close friend. A Conservator is a person who handles a minor or incapacitated person's assets. This should be a person who you feel is financially responsible. To avoid a potential conflict of interest it makes sense to appoint different people to act as Guardian and Conservator. However it may be more efficient to simply name the same person to act in each capacity. Whom you choose to appoint is up to you.

Trustee

A Trustee should be someone you believe can work well with the beneficiaries of the trust. The decision as to whom should be appointed as a Trustee is something that should be carefully considered and not made lightly.

Here is a list of some of the functions and responsibilities of a Trustee:

- The Trustee should be familiar with, and understand, the terms of the Trust
- The Trustee should be familiar with the state's trust code and state's Prudent Investor Act
- The Trustee must maintain complete and accurate records and make them available to the beneficiaries
- The Trustee should understand, and plan for, the estate, gift and generation skipping transfer tax consequences

Additionally, every Trustee has the following duties:

- The duty of skill, care and loyalty
- The duty to furnish information to, and communicate with, beneficiaries
- The duty to avoid conflicts of interest
- The duty to segregate property
- The duty of impartiality regarding current and future beneficiaries
- The duty to enforce and defend claims of the trust

Some clients choose a child or beneficiary to serve as Trustee. The main advantage to this is that they may have more familiarity with the trust assets and family dynamics. However, there are a number of disadvantages with choosing a child or beneficiary as a Trustee. One disadvantage is that a he or she is asked to perform a full-time job without the requisite knowledge of familiarity of administering a trust. Administering a trust can be very time consuming, and family members often choose not to be compensated for their time, even though the trust may allow for it. Further, any contention between the Trustee/beneficiary and other beneficiaries may fracture their personal relationships.

An Independent Trustee on the other hand is an individual who has no beneficial interest to the trust, and can include a friend, trusted advisor or Trust Company. One disadvantage to having an Independent Trustee is that he or she may charge the trust for the work performed. However, some states have laws that say that a Trustee may charge a reasonable fee for his or her services. Therefore this, coupled with the power of beneficiaries to remove a Trustee, allows for some accountability by the Trustee to perform his or her duties well and to not overcharge for their services. Furthermore, an Independent Trustee may be more objective as to the needs of the beneficiaries and may be more willing to say "No" to beneficiaries if they make unreasonable requests.

Durable Power of Attorney

This is a legal instrument by which you, as the principal, appoint another person to serve as your agent. The Durable Power of Attorney confers upon the agent authority to perform specific acts on behalf of the principal, such as the power to act in conducting the principal's business, including signing papers, checks, title documents, contracts, handling bank accounts and other activities in the name of the person granting the power. In essence, the agent can legally do anything that you can do. Therefore one of the biggest concerns people have when creating a Durable Power of Attorney is that your agent may not have your best interest at heart and may do something contrary to your wishes. One way to help protect against this is to choose an agent carefully and to pick someone who you believe will carry out your best interests.

Additionally, most Durable Powers of Attorney are effective the date they are signed. One concern that can arise from this is that if the agent has the document in hand, he or she could immediately transact business on your behalf without your knowledge. One way to alleviate this concern is by including "springing" language in the document that makes the Durable Power of Attorney valid only upon a specific occurrence, typically upon your incapacity. However, one major drawback to this is that financial institutions may want proof that you are currently incapacitated and may not rely on documentation that is only days old. One alternative to providing "springing" language is to allow the drafting attorney to hold onto the original Durable Power of Attorney and only release it to the agent upon your instruction or upon a showing that you are in fact incapacitated.

Health Care Proxy

This is a legal instrument by which you appoint an individual to make medical decisions on your behalf in the event you become incapacitated and unable to make or communicate decisions for yourself. This should be a person you believe will follow your wishes regardless of their own wishes or interests.

6

UPDATING ESTATE PLANS

Some people say that it is not enough to simply prepare an estate plan and have it sit on the shelf. It is often recommended that a person review his or her Will or Estate Plan at least every five years, or as circumstances change. Below are some circumstances which may occur in a person's life that can warrant a consideration of updating a Will or Estate Plan:

- A change in marital status
- The birth or adoption of a child
- A move to another state
- A significant change in financial status
- A significant change in tax or trust laws
- The death of a beneficiary
- A desire to add or change beneficiaries
- The death or incapacity of a named trustee or other fiduciary

Here are some additional questions to consider:

- Are you certain that your current estate plan will minimize possible state and federal estate taxes at your death?
- Have you taken steps to avoid possible will contests and disputes during the administration of your estate?
- Does your current estate plan provide creditor and lawsuit protection for assets passed to your surviving spouse and/or children?
- If you have a revocable living trust in place as part of your estate plan, is your trust fully funded so your family can avoid the delays and expenses of probate?
- Does your estate plan protect your children's inheritance in the event your surviving spouse chooses to remarry?

7

SPECIAL CONSIDERATIONS

Tricky Items to Inherit

People often hold a variety of assets or property when they pass away. Some assets are more difficult to pass down to the next generation than others. Here is a list of some of the "trickier" items:

- Vacation homes
- Artwork
- Guns
- Airline miles
- Pets
- Retirement accounts
- Items with copyrights attached to them

While many people prefer to conduct their estate planning without the use of a qualified attorney, having an attorney advise individuals on the appropriate way to distribute tricky items can help ensure the items are distributed the way the person intended.

Avoiding Litigation

Litigation in the estate planning context occurs when someone sues the estate. Some law suits can involve a creditor looking to get paid for a debt, or a family member contesting certain aspects of the estate plan. When drafting estate planning documents, there are several ways to minimize the chances of litigation over the estate.

One way is to include an "Arbitration Clause" in the Revocable Living Trust. An Arbitration Clause can require any dispute to be settled by arbitration before a neutral arbitrator instead of having to go through a lengthy court process. You can also specifically indicate things that should not be up for arbitration, such as the Settlor's competency and attempts to remove a fiduciary.

Another way to try to avoid litigation is by including an *"Interorrem Clause"* (also known as a "No Contest Clause"). A No Contest Clause provides that if a beneficiary of a Will or Trust contests the validity of the document or its provisions, the beneficiary will be treated as if he or she predeceased you without being survived by descendants. However, simply including such a clause without any "incentive" does not completely solve the problem. Therefore a number of practitioners apply the "carrot and stick" approach. For example, if you provide the person you want to disinherit something, such as a small disposition of a few thousand dollars or a percentage of the estate, then that person would have to weigh if it is worth it for them to contest the document and possibly get a greater inheritance, or risk losing what was already guaranteed to come to them in the Will or Trust.

Beneficiary Designations

Many financial instruments contain beneficiary designations that control the disposition of certain assets. These beneficiary designations typically trump the provisions of a Will or other estate planning instrument. Therefore it is critical that all beneficiary designations are updated and reflect a person's wishes and overall estate planning goals.

Assets with Beneficiary Designations:

- Individual and group life insurance
- Traditional and Roth IRAs
- Qualified retirement plans
- Employee stock option plans
- Contractual rights under deferred compensation plans
- Employment contracts

Things to Keep in Mind:

- Assign and periodically review your beneficiary designations
- Making changes to your will or your trust will not automatically make changes to all your assets listed in those documents
- Be sure to name primary and contingent beneficiaries
- When making changes to these documents, confirm with the receiving institution that the changes were actually made and reflect your wishes
- Keep copies of your beneficiary documentation

8

WILL VS. TRUST

This table compares the advantages of using a Revocable Living Trust vs. simply using a Will.

Will	Revocable Living Trust
A Will goes through Probate	A funded Trust does not go through probate
Probate is a Court process for passing title of property you own and it can be time consuming	A Trust can be considered like a business structure that allows you to control property and carry out your intent with limited court involvement
Delays of 1 year or more	The trustee has immediate control over the Trust assets of a funded Trust; there are limited delays
No estate tax savings	A funded Revocable Living Trust may minimize estate

	taxes for married couples
No protection for disabled children or disabled beneficiaries	Ongoing protection can be put in place for disabled beneficiaries
A greater chance for a contested Will or a law suit exists	Some attorneys believe that it is more difficult to attack a Trust than a Will
A child may come into an inheritance sooner than the parents would like	A Trust can limit or delay the availability of money to a child who is unable to manage an inheritance due to age or irresponsibility
A Will becomes a public record when a person dies and anyone can see it	A Trust is a private document and typically only the person making the Trust and the beneficiaries can see it

9

TAX ISSUES RELATED TO ESTATE PLANNING

Estate Planning attorneys typically counsel people on the following taxes:

- Estate Tax
- Gift Tax
- Generation Skipping Transfer Taxes

Estate Tax

An Estate Tax is a tax on your right to transfer property at your death. It consists, in basic terms, of the property you own or control when you pass away. There is both a Federal Estate Tax and a Massachusetts Estate Tax (there is no New Hampshire Estate Tax other than the Federal Estate Tax). Under the Federal Estate Tax system, a person's estate gets taxed if he or she has a taxable estate over $10 million (as adjusted for inflation). However, under the Massachusetts Estate Tax system, a person's estate gets taxed if he or she has a taxable estate over $1 million.

The following items may be includable in a person's taxable estate for Estate Tax purposes:

- All Probate Assets
- Real Estate Equity
- Retirement Plans, Annuities, Pensions
- Life Insurance in which a person has "incidents of ownership"
- Certain Business Interests
- Tangible Personal Property
- Debts owed
- UTMA account in which a person is a parent or Custodian
- Jointly held property, with certain limitations
- Property subject to Internal Revenue Code 26 USC §2036 (transfers with retained life estate) or Internal Revenue Code 26 USC §2038 (revocable transfers)
- Some gifts made within 3 years of death
- Assets held in a Revocable Trust funded by the person
- Certain assets held in Revocable Trusts
- General Powers of Appointment

Gift Tax

A person can incur Gift Tax Liability if he or she makes gifts of property during his or her lifetime. A Gift Tax is not incurred in certain situations, including:

- If a gift to an individual is below the annual exclusion amount (currently $15,000.00)
- If payments are made directly to medical and educational providers. Such payments are not considered gifts.

Generation Skipping Transfer (GST) Tax

The Generation Skipping Transfer (GST) Tax is based on the policy that the transfer of property should be taxed at least once at each generation. The Tax is based on gifts and transfers in trust to or for the benefit of unrelated persons when the recipient is more than 37.5 years younger than the person making the gift, or to related persons more than one generation younger than the donor, usually grandchildren. Please note that there are certain exceptions. Generally, GST planning is mainly a concern for high net-worth individuals, however estate planning documents for many clients include provisions related to GST issues. Any GST imposed on a transfer is in addition to any federal gift or estate taxes that may apply to the transfer.

10

NON-TAX REASONS TO HAVE AN ESTATE PLAN

As we have already discussed, Estate Planning is crucial in today's world. It allows for people to alleviate some stress from friends and family members during an extremely stressful time. In Massachusetts, one of the main reasons for a person to create a trust or estate plan is to save money on certain tax matters. However, there are various non-tax related reasons why someone should create an estate plan.

Some of the non-tax reasons to create an estate plan include:

- Asset protection of a business or real property through the creation of Trusts, entity formations, pre-marital and post-marital agreements;
- Planning for disability through the creation of a Health Care Proxy, Durable Power of Attorney and HIPAA authorizations;

- Reviewing beneficiary designation (in life insurance policies, IRAs other retirement accounts, annuities) and coordinating them with an estate plan (including an IRA Beneficiary Trust);
- Avoiding probate;
- Expressing your wishes for the transfer of your assets in a Will, beneficiary designations, or a Revocable Living Trust;
- Caring for individuals with special needs through the creation of a Special Needs Trust that may help prevent the individual from being disqualified from certain government benefits;
- Creating a structure to help a child or beneficiary who is unable to or immature enough to handle an inheritance;
- Business succession planning;
- International estate planning; and
- Pet care or animal care and succession planning through the use of a Pet Trust.

11

WAYS TO DISTRIBUTE REAL ESTATE THROUGH THE ESTATE PLANNING CONTEXT

Below is a very brief, and non-exhaustive, discussion of ways a person can distribute real estate through the estate planning context:

Gifting

A person can make a gift of real estate to another person.

- *Advantages:*
    - o Immediate ownership by another person
- *Disadvantages:*
    - o If the property has a very low basis, the person receiving the gift may have a high capital gains tax to pay upon selling the property
    - o Possible gift tax consequences

- ○ Possible generation skipping transfer tax consequences
- ○ May be considered a disqualifying transfer for Medicaid purposes and other purposes

Through a Will

A person can hold onto real estate and give it to another person when they pass away by making specific provisions in a Will.

- *Advantages:*
  - ○ A person can hold and use the property throughout his or her entire lifetime
  - ○ The property can receive a step-up in basis when a person passes real estate through a Will
- *Disadvantages:*
  - ○ The equity or value of the real estate may result in Estate Tax consequences

Through a Trust

A person can put their real estate into a Trust and have a Trustee manage the property.

- *Advantages:*
  - ○ A person can control how real estate is handled while the person is alive and can even have some control after his or her passing
  - ○ The property can receive a step-up in basis when a person passes real estate through a Grantor Trust
- *Disadvantages:*
  - ○ The equity or value of the real estate may result in Estate Tax consequences

Ways a Person Can Title Investment Real Estate

Realty Trust

A Realty Trust is a vehicle to hold legal title to real estate. The Trustees of the Realty Trust can act only with the express authority of the beneficiaries. Two main advantages for placing real estate in a Realty Trust are: 1) The beneficiaries are not listed publicly at the Registry of Deeds, thereby allowing for anonymity of ownership and privacy; and 2) Transactions involving property in Realty Trusts do not have to be recorded with the Registry of Deeds. Some of the disadvantages of placing property in a Realty Trust are that a Realty Trust does not provide any protection from creditors, transfer taxes, gift taxes or estate taxes.

Limited Liability Company (LLC)

An LLC offers protection to all members, and can limit their liability, unlike a limited partnership in which one or more general partners are liable for the entire business, and is not ordinarily subject to double taxation, unlike a subchapter C corporation. Shares of an LLC can be passed to heirs over time through gifting strategies, alleviating the tax burden of inheriting those assets all at once.

12

ADVANCE DIRECTIVES

AND HEALTH CARE DECISIONS

An Advance Directive, or a living will as it is sometimes referred to, is a set of instructions specifying what actions should be taken on your behalf if you are unable to make decisions because of illness or incapacity. Even though, as current law stands, such a document is not legally binding in Massachusetts, it does provide your Health Care Agent with some guidance as to what your feelings are about these sensitive matters.

It is important to note that the United States Supreme Court has made it clear in *Cruzan v. Missouri* that there must be "clear and convincing" evidence expressing a person's wishes for removal of life support. Without that expression, such as that in an Advance Directive, a state court may require you to be kept alive through whatever means are necessary.

Here are some things to consider when preparing an Advance Directive:

- Should extraordinary measures be taken to keep you alive?
- What kind of quality of life do you find acceptable?
- What are your wishes in regards to administering pain relief medication?
- Do you want to donate your organs?
- Do you have any specific religious wishes you want expressed?

Having your wishes stated ahead of time can make things a bit easier for your family during a difficult time.

13
529 PLANS VS. CRUMMEY TRUST

529 Plan

Often, parents and grandparents are looking for ways to pay for a child's or grandchild's education. A 529 Plan can provide income tax advantages if the assets are used for higher education. Such a plan allows you to remain in control of your assets during your lifetime and, at the same time, have the assets removed from your estate for estate tax purposes. For people who want to have control during their life, yet have estate tax concerns, this is something to consider.

A 529 Plan qualifies for the annual gift tax exclusion, and with a certain election, it may qualify for the use of up to five years of exclusion. That means that a donor may make a contribution of $70,000 completely excluded from the gift tax. In addition to gifting to a 529 Plan, donors may give an unlimited amount for tuition if paid directly to an educational institution.

Crummey Trust

Sometimes people do not want to gift directly to their child or grandchild, but want to keep the assets in trust. An irrevocable trust with *"Crummey"* withdrawal powers can be an effective way to obtain the annual gift tax exclusion even though the gift is in trust.

An Irrevocable Gift Giving Trust (also known as a *Crummey* Trust, named for the court case it became famous for) is a trust designed to allow someone to irrevocably give away assets to named beneficiaries, usually children. The assets (or at least the appreciation thereon) can thereby be excluded from the person's estate, and will be invested and paid to the beneficiaries in accordance with the trust provisions. A so-called *Crummey* power is generally included so that the gifts, when made, will constitute gifts of a present interest and thereby qualify for the annual gift tax exclusion.

The choice of whether to focus on a 529 Plan or a *Crummey* Trust is one that should be carefully considered based on your specific situation and appropriate financial and legal advice.

14

CHARITABLE CONTRIBUTIONS
AND PLANNED GIVING

Often, people wonder what the best way is to make a charitable contribution. Planned Giving is one way in which a person can make a charitable contribution. Planned Giving may be done in line with a person's financial plans or through his or her estate plan through the use of certain instruments.

Types of Planned Giving Instruments

- *Will or Revocable Living* Trust – Through a Will or Revocable Living Trust, a person can leave a specific gift to a charity that takes effect upon the person's death.
- *Charitable Gift* Annuity – A Charitable Gift Annuity is a contract between a person and a charity whereby the charity agrees to pay a fixed amount of money to an individual for his or her lifetime in exchange for a transfer of assets.

- *Charitable Remainder* Trust – A Charitable Remainder Trust pays a person and/or another beneficiary income for life and provides a substantial charitable income tax deduction. A person can choose either a fixed income or a set percentage of the value of the Trust, determined annually.
- *Charitable Lead* Trust – A Charitable Lead Trust gives a charity income for a set number of years but retains the principal for person's heirs.

Types of Assets to Leave to a Charity

One important consideration is that if assets will not be left until death, assets which consist of Income in Respect to a Decedent ("IRD"), like an IRA, make good assets to leave to charity. IRD assets do not get a step-up in basis at the death of the taxpayer. But, a charity will not pay tax on the IRD asset, while a non-charitable beneficiary would pay tax. Thus, an IRD asset is worth more to a charity than it is to a non-charitable beneficiary.

15

SPECIAL NEEDS TRUSTS

A Supplemental or Special Needs Trust is an Estate Planning tool that is used to allow a disabled person to receive certain funds without affecting his eligibility for "needs based" public benefit programs (i.e., programs that set limits on the amount of assets and income a person can have). The purpose of the Trust is to invest and manage the Trust assets for the benefit of the disabled person in a way that does not interfere with the person's eligibility for these government benefits.

Self-Settled Special Needs Trust vs. Third Party Special Needs Trust

A Self-Settled Special Needs Trust is one that is set up by the disabled person (or by someone acting on his or her behalf) with his own funds. This type of Trust is useful if the disabled person obtains an inheritance or wins the lottery, and the receipt of this money would otherwise make him ineligible for certain public benefits. When this Trust is terminated, the remaining Trust assets typically go back to the State to repay them for the services that were used under a payback provision.

A Third Party Special Needs Trust is set up by someone other than the disabled person (usually a parent). This is a purely discretionary Trust that makes no obligations to pay funds to the disabled person, and is used to supplement, but not supplant, benefits and services the person is eligible to receive. The Trust is discretionary in order to prevent any payback requirement to the State. So if a parent sets up this Trust for a child, they can indicate that the Trust Funds can supplement the services the disabled person receives, and once the disabled person dies, the Trust funds do not go back to the State, but are distributed the way the parent intended.

SSI Guidelines and the Role of the Trustee

Supplemental Security Income (SSI) is a federal program that provides cash benefits to blind, disabled, and aged individuals. In order to be eligible for SSI, a person must have less than $2,000 in countable assets and a low income. The Trusts are used to give additional funds to the disabled person that are not covered by SSI (as long as the funds are not used for food or shelter). The goal is to keep the disabled person's income as low as possible to keep him eligible for SSI. (Please note, however, that there are some instances where it is desirable to give the disabled person additional funds that would reduce the SSI benefits.) SSI has many different ways of calculating income, but the two basic ways are "Direct Income" and "In-Kind Income." Direct Income is cash or money received by the disabled person, and it will reduce the SSI benefits on a dollar-for-dollar basis. In-Kind Income is when something other than money is received, and as long as it is not a payment for food or shelter, it should be considered an exempt asset and should not be counted as income that would reduce eligibility.

There are a couple of ways to allowably distribute In-Kind Income. One is by the Trustee personally purchasing the goods with Trust money and delivering it directly to the disabled person. The other way is by making a payment directly to the provider who then gives the goods to the disabled person. The point is for the Trustee to give the disabled beneficiary items that cannot be converted to cash and are not considered food or shelter.

The following expenditures can be made without causing a reduction to the disabled person's SSI payment:

- Cable Television
- Computer equipment
- Curtains, towels, linens
- Entertainment expenses
- Expenses related to owning and operating one car
- Furniture and household items
- Gifts
- Guardianship and advocacy services
- Health Club/YMCA memberships
- Home appliances
- Home renovations to improve accessibility
- Independent evaluations
- Insurance premiums
- Interior decorating
- Internet access
- Medical equipment
- Medical, nursing and dental care not otherwise provided for
- Medications
- Newspaper and magazine subscriptions
- Office supplies
- Personal assistance/coaching
- School or camp tuition
- Telephone service
- Tickets to sporting events/theatre, etc.
- Therapists, tutors, teachers
- Travel expenses such as transportation

- Vacations (but not hotel accommodations, as that may be considered shelter)
- Veterinary services, pet care and supplies

The Social Security Administration (SSA) has considered the following items to be considered as food and shelter which the Trustee should not pay for:

- Electricity
- Food
- Garbage removal
- Gas
- Heating fuel
- Mortgage and property insurance required by the mortgage holder
- Real Property taxes
- Rent
- Sewer
- Water

The SSI program requires periodic reports for all SSI recipients. The representative Payee must report the existence of the Self-Settled Special Needs Trust to the SSA. Additionally, the following things must be reported to the SSA regarding the disabled person within 10 days after the end of the month in which the event occurred:

- A change in his address, employment status or living arrangement
- A change in his income and countable resources
- New eligibility for other benefits
- A change in his health insurance coverage
- Medical improvements
- A change in his marital status
- Admission to or discharge from any heath facility or public facility (such as a hospital or nursing home)

- His taking a trip outside the United States

The report should be in writing and include the disabled person's name, Social Security number, the name of the person preparing the report and a description of the event that resulted in a report needing to be filed.

Additional Information

- The Trustees should preserve all financial records, including bank and investment statements, checks and invoices.
- Bank accounts and other Trust investments should be in the names of the Trustees. Example: Ray G. Price, Trustee of the Frank G. Price Special Needs Trust u/a/d August 1, 2012 (u/a/d means under agreement dated).
- The Trust must file an income tax return each year and it must receive its own tax identification number. If income is distributed to a beneficiary, the Trust will issue the beneficiary a "K-1" and the income will be taxed to the beneficiary rather than to the Trust.

16
REP PAYEE AND VA FIDUCIARIES

A government agency may appoint someone to manage income benefits for a person who needs help managing those benefits. The Social Security Administration calls the person who is appointed a Representative Payee (Rep Payee), and The Department of Veterans Affairs calls the appointee a VA Fiduciary.

These individuals have authority to manage the benefit checks of the Agency. The Rep Payee and VA Fiduciary have no legal authority to manage other property, financial affairs, or medical matters for the protected person. To control other matters, the fiduciary must have legal authority from another source, such as through a power of attorney, trust, or court appointment.

The responsibilities of a Rep Payee and VA Fiduciary include the following:

- Avoid conflicts of interest

- Make sure the protected person's day-to-day needs for food, clothing and shelter are met
- Pay bills on time
- Keep a detailed accounting of funds received and funds paid
- Adhere to any special reporting requirements
- Protect unspent funds
- Do not comingle funds

Please note that a Rep Payee or VA Fiduciary can contact the agency directly for additional assistance.

17
WHAT TO DO WHEN YOU KNOW YOU ARE DYING

When someone knows that their time on this earth is coming to an end, they are overcome with a number of emotions. They often reflect on their lives and the road that led them to where they are now. They often realize that this time can also be difficult for their family, so they look for a way to help ease the burden on the family by "getting their affairs in order." Below is a brief and non-exhaustive discussion of some things a person should consider as they prepare for death.

Legal Affairs

Meeting with an attorney to get your final legal affairs in order makes a lot of sense. The attorney can help you create a Will and/or Trust so your property gets passed down at death the way you intended. The attorney can also look at other questions involving title to property that may be in dispute.

Be Hospital/Hospice Ready

- Prepare a list of medications
- Have a copy of necessary medical records and medical history
- Bring a copy of the Health Care Proxy, HIPAA Release, Advance Directive and Durable Power of Attorney

Other Things to Consider

- Palliative care through Hospice
- What you would like your last words to be
- What you would like to hear the moment you are passing
- Prepare a Funeral and Burial Directions document that indicates your wishes upon your passing

18

CHECKLIST OF THINGS TO DO WHEN A PERSON PASSES AWAY

When a loved one passes away, the details that need to be taken care of by his or her friends and family members may be overwhelming, especially during such an emotional time. The following checklist is intended to help friends and family members keep track of some of the matters that will need to be tended to.

Things to Do Following a Person's Death

- Get a legal pronouncement of death. If no doctor is present, then someone will need to be contacted to do this:
  - o If the person dies at home under hospice care, the hospice nurse will need to be called because he or she can declare the death and help facilitate the transportation of the body
  - o If the person dies at home without hospice care, 911 should be called and a do-not-resuscitate document should be in hand if it

exists. Without one, paramedics will generally start emergency procedures and, except where permitted to pronounce death, take the person to an emergency room for a doctor to make the declaration

- Arrange for transportation of the body. If no autopsy is needed, the body can be picked up by a mortuary or crematorium
- Notify the person's doctor or the county coroner
- Handle the care of dependents and pets
- Arrange for a funeral or memorial service. Find out what the decedent's wishes were regarding his or her funeral or memorial service
- Contact friends and family members and let them know about the funeral or memorial arrangements
- Determine if all or part of the decedent's funeral costs have been prepaid. Often, a person has documentation indicating whether they have any prepaid agreements with a funeral home or if the decedent had a prepaid plot and/or burial insurance
- If the decedent was a veteran, the Veterans Administration should be contacted because they may be able to help with some of the costs. In addition, it is possible that veterans may be buried in a national cemetery and may be able to receive a ceremonial American flag, headstone and a Presidential memorial certificate
- Submit an obituary to the decedent's local newspapers
- Keep track of all donations, flowers, and cards received
- Secure the decedent's real estate and notify the decedent's home owner's insurance
- Secure the decedent's tangible personal property, such as silverware, dishes, furniture, or artwork. In the coming months, the Personal Representative will need to have these items appraised and distributed according to the decedent's wishes. This may be a difficult task if the property has already been distributed to various family

members. The Personal Representative is responsible for filing an inventory and appraisal of the decedent's assets with the probate court

- Notify the post office and use the forward mail option
- Notify the local Social Security office if the funeral director has not already done so
- Notify the decedent's health insurance company
- Notify life insurance companies
- Look into employment benefits by contacting the decedent's employer
- Terminate other insurance policies that are no longer necessary
- Make a list of important bills and continue to make mortgage payments if appropriate
- Notify the decedent's attorney, financial advisor and accountant

Documents to Obtain

- Death certificates (10-15 certified copies)
- Social Security card
- Marriage certificate
- Insurance policies
- Deeds and titles to property
- Automobile title and registration papers
- Stock certificates
- Bank passbooks
- Honorable discharge papers for a veteran and/or VA claim number
- Recent income tax forms and W-2 forms
- Loan and installment payment books and contracts
- Will, Trust and other estate planning documents

19

WHAT HAPPENS WHEN A PERSON DIES WITHOUT A WILL?

When a person passes away, his or her ownership of certain property ends and the title of that property needs to be transferred to someone else. A person can prepare a Will or Trust to specifically designate how this property will be passed down. However, if a person passes away without a Will or Trust, or the documents do not dispose of certain property, the property will be distributed pursuant to state law. Please note that this is only a partial list.

Section 2-102 of the Massachusetts Uniform Probate Code

Share of Spouse

The intestate share of a decedent's surviving spouse is:

  (1) the entire intestate estate if:
       (i)   no descendant or parent of the decedent survives the decedent; or

      (ii) all of the decedent's surviving descendants are also descendants of the surviving spouse and there is no other descendant of the surviving spouse who survives the decedent;

(2) the first $200,000, plus 3/4 of any balance of the intestate estate, if no descendant of the decedent survives the decedent, but a parent of the decedent survives the decedent;

(3) the first $100,000 plus 1/2 of any balance of the intestate estate, if all of the decedent's surviving descendants are also descendants of the surviving spouse and the surviving spouse has 1 or more surviving descendants who are not descendants of the decedent;

(4) the first $100,000 plus 1/2 of any balance of the intestate estate, if 1 or more of the decedent's surviving descendants are not descendants of the surviving spouse.

Section 2-103 of the Massachusetts Uniform Probate Code

Share of Heirs Other Than Surviving Spouse

Any part of the intestate estate not passing to the decedent's surviving spouse under section 2-102, or the entire intestate estate if there is no surviving spouse, passes in the following order to the individuals designated below who survive the decedent:

(1) to the decedent's descendants per capita at each generation;

(2) if there is no surviving descendant, to the decedent's parents equally if both survive, or to the surviving parent;

(3) if there is no surviving descendant or parent, to the descendants of the decedent's parents or either of them per capita at each generation;

(4) if there is no surviving descendant, parent, or descendant of a parent, then equally to the decedent's next of kin in equal degree; but if there are two or more descendants of deceased ancestors in equal degree claiming through different ancestors, those claiming through the nearest ancestor shall be preferred to those claiming through an ancestor more remote. Degrees of kindred shall be computed according to the rules of civil law.

Section 2-105 of the Massachusetts Uniform Probate Code

No Taker

If there is no taker under the provisions of this article, the intestate estate passes to the Commonwealth of Massachusetts, unless the intestate is a veteran who died while a member of the Soldiers' Home in Massachusetts or the Soldiers' Home in Holyoke. In those cases, the intestate estate shall inure to the benefit of the legacy fund or legacy account of the soldiers' home of which the intestate was a member.

Non-Probate Property

Furthermore, property held in a person's name alone can either be considered probate property or non-probate property. If certain property can pass title automatically, then the property does not need to be probated, and property held in joint ownership passes to the joint owner.

Non-probate property includes, but is not limited to:
- Real and Personal Property held in joint tenancy
- Life insurance with beneficiary designation provisions
- Payable on death (POD) or transfer on death (TOD) contracts
- Interests in Trust
- Accounts with beneficiary designation provisions

If There is a Surviving Spouse for a New Hampshire Resident

If there is a surviving spouse, then the estate passes in the following manner:

- The surviving spouse receives the entire estate if the decedent had no surviving parent or child;
- The surviving spouse receives the first $250,000 of the estate plus one-half the balance if there is a surviving child of both the decedent and the surviving spouse, and there are no other children of the surviving spouse who survive the decedent;
- The surviving spouse receives the first $250,000 plus three-fourths of the balance if there is a surviving parent of the decedent, but no surviving child;
- The surviving spouse receives the first $150,000, plus one-half of the balance of the estate if there is a surviving child of both the decedent and the surviving spouse and the surviving spouse has a surviving child who is not the child of the decedent;
- The surviving spouse receives $100,000 and one-half of the estate, if the decedent left children who are not also children of the surviving spouse.

If There is No Surviving Spouse for a New Hampshire Resident

If there is no surviving spouse, or if parts of the intestate estate still have not been distributed under the above formula, then the remainder of the estate passes in the following order:

- To the children of the decedent, in equal shares;
- If the decedent has no surviving children, then to the parent(s) of the decedent;
- If the decedent has no surviving children or parent(s), then to the surviving brothers and sisters of the decedent in equal shares and to the children of the decedent's deceased brothers and sisters by

representation. (Representation means that these children share equally the portion their parent would have received had their parent survived the decedent.);

- If the decedent has no surviving children, parent(s), or brothers or sisters, or children of deceased brothers or sisters then, to grandparent(s);
- If there are no surviving children, parent, children of a parent, or grandparent, but there are children of decedent's grandparent who survive, one-half of the estate passes to the children of the paternal grandparent who are not beyond the fourth degree of kinship to the decedent; the other half passes to the children of the maternal grandparent who are not beyond the fourth degree of kinship; provided, however, that if there are no children of the decedent's grandparent within the fourth degree of kinship to the decedent on either the paternal or maternal side, the entire estate passes to the issue on the other side who are not beyond the fourth degree of kinship to the decedent.

No portion of a person's intestate estate shall pass to any person who is of the fifth or greater degree of kinship to the decedent. If no one is available to take the estate under the provisions of the intestacy law, the intestate estate passes to the State of New Hampshire by a process called "escheat."

Also, children born of unwed parents inherit through their mother, but can also inherit through their father if the father acknowledges paternity or is found to be the father through a court proceeding.

20
ESTATE PLANNING AND TECHNOLOGY

All too often I come across a situation where a client has gone through the entire process of putting together a great estate plan but fails to take the final steps necessary to make things easier for the family. It's not enough to just go through the process and create a great estate plan and then do nothing with it. After all, what's the point of just leaving it in your lawyer's desk drawer?

Accessing important information

I always recommend that my clients keep physical copies of all of their important estate planning documents and to keep them easily accessible for the family members who might need them in the future. A person can keep all of this information, including other important financial information, in a binder that is accessible when a client passes away or is incapacitated. This binder should also include information dealing with desired funeral and burial directions so that the family knows exactly what the client wanted to have done. You can even consider keeping a Wallet ID card that contains the names and contact information of your health care proxy and other emergency information, including any allergies or a lists of medications you take. You might also consider storing your information electronically, using a computer or a mobile device.

Accessing important information from the Cloud

One of my favorite methods of storing information is through Cloud Computing on a mobile device. "The Cloud" refers to software and services that run and are stored on the internet. There are a number of different Cloud services, including Google Drive, Apple iCloud, Dropbox and Microsoft Office 365.

I recommend Google Drive because of its user friendly format. Google Drive is a file storage and synchronization service. It allows you to store files, share files and edit documents all in the Cloud. If you have a Google account, you can access your Google Drive information anywhere you have an internet connection simply by logging into your Google Account. So if you upload something onto Google Drive from your computer, you can then access that same information from your mobile device, and vice versa. With Google Drive you can even store and access all of your health care information in one spot and access it whenever and wherever you need it.

So here is how it might play out. You end up going to the hospital or the ER and the doctors need your list of medications and health history in order to properly treat you. If you had that information stored on your mobile device you can share that information right then and there with your doctors. But what happens if you are unconscious? If you are unconscious, you will obviously not be unable to share that information. However, if you stored that information on your Google Drive, and then shared that information with a spouse or loved one, they in turn have access to the information that the doctors may desperately need in order to treat you properly.

You should also consider uploading your health care proxy, advance directive and other relevant estate planning documents on your Google Drive. It also makes sense to share this information with your health care proxy. After all, they are the ones you appoint to make health care decisions on your behalf, so why not allow them to have access to all your relevant health care data? There are privacy concerns for you to be aware of, but if you are satisfied with it, then saving such information on the Cloud can be a huge benefit.

21
OLD SCHOOL MEETS NEW SCHOOL

Back in the day, estate planning documents were very difficult to read and full of legalese and Latin phrases. Over the last few years there has been a trend in the law to move away from such language to more plain English. There is also a trend toward making documents easily amendable. It used to be that if you wanted to make small changes to a document, you would have to redo the entire document because everything was so intertwined. Now, some attorneys set up their documents in a paragraph form that makes it easy to cut and paste paragraphs when changes need to be made, thereby saving the client time and money.

Other ways estate planning has joined the 21st century is by how easy it is for attorneys and clients to share information. After an Estate Plan is completed, an attorney can scan the documents and then e-mail the information to the client or even create a client portal whereby the attorney and client freely share and review information relevant to the client's file.

22

ONLINE AND DIGITAL ACCOUNTS WORKSHEET

It used to be that when a person passed away, the Personal Representative would be advised to wait by the mail box and look for any mail that would indicate what assets the deceased person owned. However, as our society has increasingly become paperless, it is becoming more difficult to have an easily identifiable paper trail of a person's assets. And without such a paper trail, it can be very difficult for the Personal Representative to locate what assets a person actually owned.

In Massachusetts as well as other states, the law relating to online accounts for a deceased or incapacitated person is not clear. Therefore it should be assumed that a Personal Representative or Attorney-In-Fact will not have access to these accounts. Therefore it is strongly recommended that you keep a written list of all your online accounts as well as a list of all bills and documents you receive in paperless form. This will make things easier for your Personal Representative or Attorney-In-

Fact under your Durable Power of Attorney. You should consider keeping this list with the rest of your Estate Planning documents.

You should strongly consider backing up the information contained in the online accounts (e.g. financial statements, real estate documents ,pictures, music, etc.) in a format that is easily accessible upon your passing or incapacitation.

You may also want to keep a separate list of all your username and passwords along with the answers to the secret questions in a safe and secure place for your own benefit. **Please Note** that some online accounts may not allow you to share your username and password, therefore you must read the terms of service for accounts you have established in order to determine whether the information can be transferred or accessed by others.

Additionally, your Personal Representative may need to notify certain service providers of your passing and your Personal Representative may also need to stop all automatic payments from being made. Therefore updating and maintaining the list regularly will help your Personal Representative.

Here is a sample Online and Digital Accounts Worksheet:

Name of Online Account	Purpose the Account Is Used For

(Some of the Online Accounts you may wish to list on this worksheet include Facebook, Twitter, Shutterfly, iTunes, Verizon/Comcast, Bank Accounts, Brokerage Accounts, Financial Accounts, Merchandise Accounts, E-mail Accounts, Websites, Blogs, Online Accounts that provide you with Paperless Statements and any other online Account you may have)

23

CONCLUSION

Estate planning, as you have learned by reading this book, is not as simple as making out a will and keeping it in a safe place.

There are many things to take into consideration, from whether to put part of your estate in a trust to how to store your documents on the Cloud.

Despite all the issues you need to weigh, estate planning can be a relatively straightforward process. I hope that this treatise has helped you understand not only the importance of proper planning but the steps you need to take to ensure that your estate will be handled properly after you pass away.

I'd like to remind you, once again, that this book is designed not to be a do-it-yourself guide to estate planning but, rather, an overview of the issues you should consider when discussing your estate with an experienced attorney who handles estate planning.

ABOUT THE AUTHOR

Attorney Peter A. Moustakis founded Moustakis Law LLC in 2011 and joined forces with Sowerby Law Office, PLLC in 2020 to form Sowerby & Moustakis Law, PLLC. The firm is committed to helping families through different legal matters as their lives unfold. Whether it is through the purchase of a new home, the preparation of a Will or dealing with the loss of a loved one, Sowerby & Moustakis Law, PLLC is committed to providing the legal counsel necessary.

Peter understands the responsibility and trust that comes with representing a person through what is often the most difficult time in his or her life. He considers himself a true "Counselor-at-law" whose purpose is to provide his clients with guidance and an understanding of the law. Peter strives to establish a client-oriented practice that focuses on listening and empathizing with clients while also helping them sort through their issues and concerns. His law firm has grown over the last few years and he is excited to see the practice continue to grow.

Peter A. Moustakis graduated from New England Law | Boston where he attended the night program in order to work as a paralegal during the day. While attending law school, he was awarded the honor of New England Scholar and achieved the Cali Excellence for the Future Award for his excellence in Estate Planning. Peter has also contributed to two Family Law publications.

Peter enjoys volunteering in his local community, woodworking and various equine activities. He is supported by his loving wife and family who helped make this book possible.